# LEARN THE VALUE OF

# Cooperation

◆

by ELAINE P. GOLEY

Illustrated by Debbie Crocker

◆

ROURKE ENTERPRISES, INC.

VERO BEACH, FL 32964

**Library of Congress Cataloging-in-Publication Data**

Goley, Elaine P., 1949–
    Learn the value of cooperation.

    Summary: Examines the meaning of cooperation
and its importance in day-to-day life.
    1. Cooperation (Ethics)—Juvenile literature.
[1. Cooperativeness.]  I. Title.  II. Title: Cooperation.
    BJ1474.G64    1988    170'.2'0222—dc19    88-35317
    ISBN 0-86592-390-6

# Cooperation

Do you know what **cooperation** is?

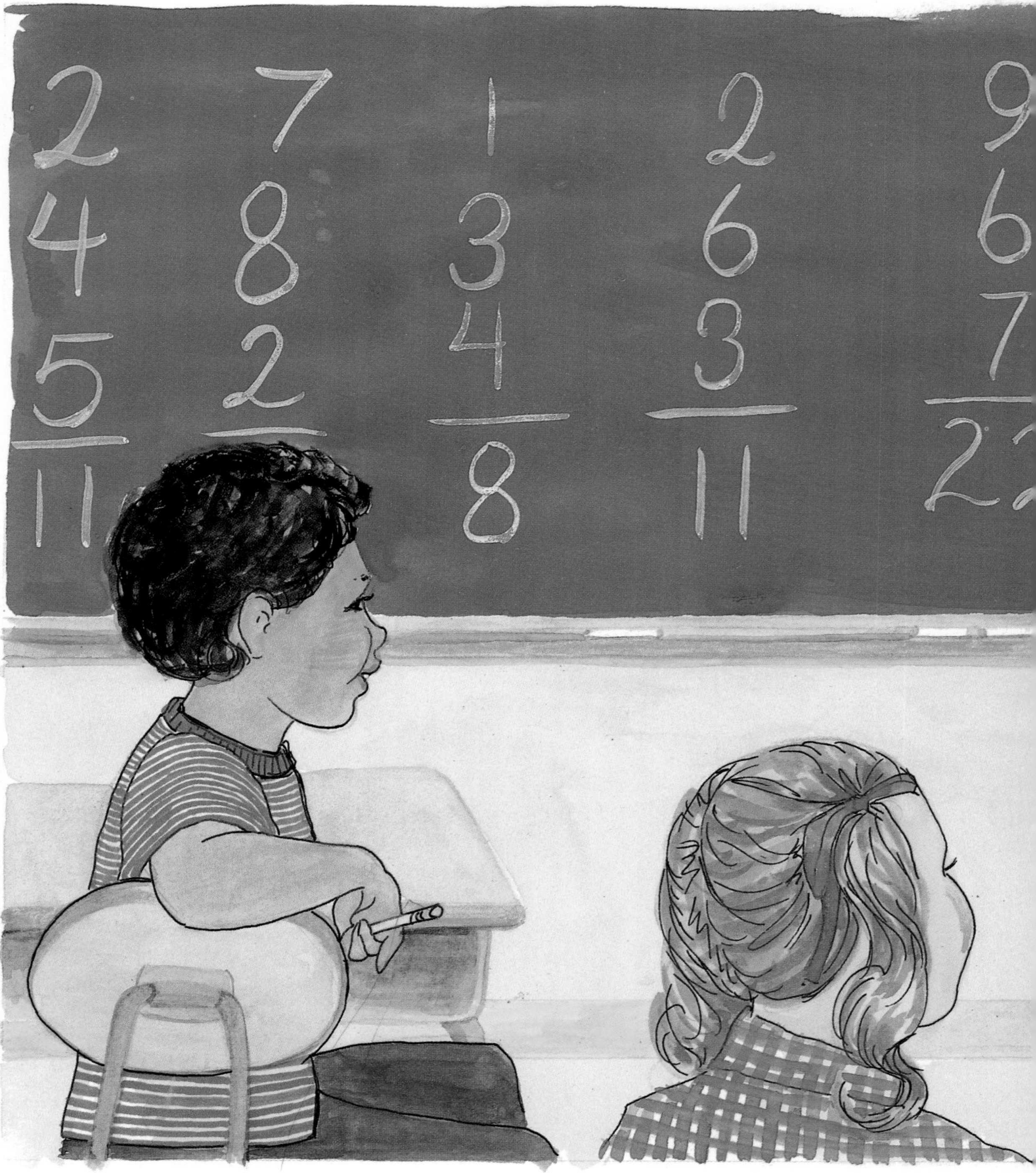
2 4 5 11
7 8 2
1 3 4 8
2 6 3 11
9 6 7 2

When you are quiet in class so your teacher
can show you how to do a math problem,
you're **cooperating.**

**Cooperation** is helping your parents clean the house by vacuuming the floor.

**Cooperation** is putting your dad's tools away after you use them so that he can find them again.

Helping your brother make his kite is **cooperating.**

You're **cooperating** when you put trash in the proper container after you eat lunch at school.

**Cooperation** is waiting for your turn at bat
when you play baseball.

Working together on the school play takes **cooperation.**
Some paint scenery, and others have a part in the play,
but each person makes an important contribution.

Helping your little sister get dressed in the morning
so she won't be late for school is **cooperating.**

**Cooperation** is teamwork—many people working together for a football team to score.

It takes **cooperation** for a sailboat to sail . . .

. . . and for a choir to sing.

Helping your neighbor pick up trash to keep
the neighborhood clean is **cooperation.**

You **cooperate** when you put your clean clothes in your dresser.

When our family gets together for a picnic,
everyone **cooperates** by doing his job so the
whole family can enjoy food and games.

**Cooperation** is working together—like having
a bake sale to raise money for the class trip to the zoo.

We have to **cooperate** to plan a birthday party for Mom. She'll be so surprised!

Working with others makes you feel happy
and proud of the things we can do together when
we **cooperate** . . . like making a model of the
Liberty Bell for our class history project.

Helping your father get the job done is **cooperation.**

# Cooperation

"Help!" called Judy.

Judy's mom heard her and ran outside to help. Before long, an ambulance pulled into Judy's driveway. When Judy came back from the hospital, she was in a wheelchair. Judy had a broken leg and a broken arm.

"I won't be able to play with my friends for a long time," cried Judy. "How will I ever do my schoolwork?"

Rring! Judy's mom answered the door. Three of Judy's friends came in.

"I got a new video," said Alice. "We could watch it together."

"Don't worry about your homework," said Helen. "I'll bring it to you."

"And I'll walk your dog in the morning and after school," said Eva.

"Thanks. With all this help, I'll be well in no time," said Judy.


How did Judy's friends show **cooperation?** What would you do if Judy were your friend?

# Cooperation

It was almost Thanksgiving day. Mrs. Gould's class was planning a play.

"I want to be an Indian," said Tom

"I'll be a Pilgrim," said Mike.

"I'll sew costumes," said Anne.

"We need a stuffed paper turkey for the Thanksgiving feast scene," said Diane. "Would you like to make it for us, Blair?"

"No, I don't want to be a part of this silly play," answered Blair.

"Come on," everyone said.

"Oh, OK," said Blair, "I'll do it."

It was the day of the play. All was going well. Now it was time for the Thanksgiving scene. The Indians and Pilgrims were on stage.

"And now we'll eat the turkey," said Pete in a loud voice.

Everyone waited for Blair to bring the turkey on stage. He never came.

What happened to the play because Blair didn't **cooperate?**

How do you **cooperate** with others?